Online business

Starting an online business

THE ULTIMATE GUIDE ON STARTING AN

ONLINE BUSINESS FAST

By

Erik Penders

www.erikpenders.com

Introduction

I've put everything I've learned in 10 years as an internet marketer, in a practical format. Useable by anyone, for anyone, in any market and for any product or service. All written down in an easy to understand guide, even if you have zero experience.

If you want to build an online business and promote, market or sell something online, this is it. You do not need anything else.

If you know me, you know I teach others how to create 'lifestyle businesses'. This basically means creating a business that supports your lifestyle. Instead of the other way around.

Trust me when I say that anyone can create freedom for themselves if they set their mind to it. Learn, apply and take action. I will show you the way, you take the action.

We will go in to detail where it's needed, but every single part of this format can be a whole book on itself. Although I cannot cover every subject in detail, you will have all the vital information you need.

You will become an internet marketing professional with this book alone and you will be equipped to start your own online empire.

I've always had a soft spot for online business, because I believe it to be immensely powerful. You can reach millions of people with a single click of your mouse.
The digital world is getting more and more crowded these days, so it's harder to stand out from the crowd. At least that's what many internet marketers want you to believe.

I disagree. The fact that the internet is getting more crowded, doesn't mean it's harder to stand out. Yes competition is rising, but most of the competition is missing the point when it comes to effective marketing and building a business.

I truly believe it's actually a good thing that the internet is so crowded. A lot of people will disagree with me, but I think it's not that much harder to stand out from the crowd nowadays.

Add the right kind of value, to the right kind of market and you've already beaten 90% of the competition in that market.

It's all about adding value, it's not rocket science. If you want to market something to a specific group or in a specific niche, think about the problems they face and how you can help solve them.

This should be the basis of everything you do online. If you stick to that mindset, you will succeed.

Next to this mindset you need knowledge about internet business and a plan. The information and plan you need is right here. It's the result of 10 years of experience, trial and error and connecting the dots. If you bring the mindset and take action, you'll be up and running in no time.

My main goal with this book is to teach you how to start an online business in a way that's fast but right to the point.

You will learn the most important factors of marketing online and how to use these factors. We'll be going through the whole basis of an online business, step by step.

Next to that, I'll share what I believe to be the best and fastest strategy to start an online business. With no experience, no knowledge, starting from scratch.

Before we start I want to let you that if you need help on any of these topics, feel free to send me an email at info@erikpenders.com. I'll be glad to help you out. Let me share a little bit more about me, so you understand where I'm coming from.

About the writer

I'm a dutch internet marketer. I've founded two business in the Netherlands and I managed to create good income with them.

Which is fine, but it wasn't really what I wanted in the end. They soaked up most of my time and if there was one thing I wanted it was FREEDOM.

I feel that online business is by far the best and most viable way to do that. I call these businesses 'lifestyle businesses'.

They are build to support your lifestyle and create the freedom you want. The moment I ran into online business, I was so amazed by the possibilities, that I knew this was what I wanted. Right now I'm a full time online entrepreneur with one main goal.

Besides (logically) keep making passive income and creating freedom for myself, I really want to share the amazing (and sometimes very simple) opportunities online with you.

I want to show you how you can do exactly the same as I did. You can do this on any topic, subject, talent or interest. Making money online and creating (passive) income feels amazing and it can be much easier than you think.

Don't get me wrong, it's not easy. You need to do the hard work, but if you are committed and you take action, you will find it's quite simple. It's about solving problems and creating value. There is not easier way to create this value than online.

I'm telling you, the moment you decide this 'online thing' can be a real business you'll be making money in no time. I can honestly say it's not that hard.

That doesn't mean it doesn't take any real effort, it does. Every entrepreneur knows, there are no shortcuts and online business is no different. You have to put in the hours.

If you do that, it can be very rewarding. By all means, go for it! I will help you succeed, that my passion. I love all the success stories and I love help creating them.

I'm very serious about helping you and I'll teach you everything you need to know. If you would like to learn more, please go to my website http://www.erikpenders.com.

Sign up for my 'tactical Tuesday' newsletter and you'll see how I do it and how you can copy these strategies.

Anyone can do this, seriously. I will show you which amazing opportunities are waiting for you and how you can start or improve your business. I hope to see you there and talk to you soon. (This is not an empty promise, I will be there and you will get help from me. Not an assistant or intern, just me.)

A product or service to sell

On creating and/or finding a product

If you want to start in internet marketing or online business, you need something to sell. I made the mistake in the past to have a nice blog and put all the marketing together, but never really thought about what I could sell.

Luckily there are plenty of products to be found or created. It's really not that hard these days. You can go for the 'easy' route and sell existing products or services and get paid commission on them. Or the slightly 'harder' route and create your own products.

Which one is best for you is hard to say. If you want to start fast and start earning money fast, existing products is the best choice. You will be an 'affiliate' and promote products someone else created.

You get paid a commission when you make a sell. This commission can go up as high as 80%. Don't worry if you have no clue how this works, I'll show you.

If you want to go for a more sustainable long term strategy, you should always consider creating your own products. In the end, it's much better to build a growing and sustainable business. If you want to start as an affiliate and do this later, that's absolutely possible. But the first step in your online (lifestyle) business is this:

Step 1: Create or find a product or service to sell

Sounds great, but with no internet experience how do you do this? You might be surprised but it's very easy. Let me show you some great options to get a product. I'll explain how to market and sell the product later.

Perhaps you already have an existing business, maybe local or online. That means you already have services or products to sell, great. Than you can skip the next part and go straight to marketing and selling those services/ products.

Creating products

Creating products is challenging I must admit. Especially high quality ones. But, if you put some serious time and effort in it, it's well worth your time. Here are four great options for creating products yourself:

- **Write a book**

What am I talking about? You're probably not a writer right? Well, nor was I. I never wrote a word in my life. But here you are, reading this book right? I found out that a book can be as long or as short as you want. If you add value, if it helps people, it doesn't have to be long.

Besides that, most 'longer' books often beat around the bush for a long time and don't get to the point until page 723. Why is that? Isn't it a shame if the reader misses out on that great value on page 723? Just because it took them ages to reach it? Why not write a short book, to the point and directive?

It's a misconception that longer books are better books. It's just not necessarily true. So think about it for a second. Is there something you are good at? Can you write like 500 words a day? This means you can create a valuable book within a week! You can upload it to kindle, Createspace or sell it as an ebook on your website.

Although this might feel like a challenge at first, remember what it's about. You don't have to be a 'fancy' writer or have professional writing skills. It's about value value value. If you have something to say or teach, you can put it in a book.

Even if that book will not be perfect. Heck, I believe most or my products are not even near perfect. But I got over it. Because I know there is value in them. I know it can help people. Why wouldn't you be able to do the same?

I think this is one of the easiest products to create. Even if you have no experience in writing. And listen, you might think you have no talents or skills to share, but you do. People are constantly looking for help on subjects, all subjects! From plants, to animals, to the physical body, the mind, relationships, gardening, hiking, seriously anything.

"Never underestimate what you have to offer"

We tend to tell ourselves we are not that special. Who would listen to what we have to say right? Well, a lot of people. We are all different and we've all learned different things at different times. I'm 100% sure there is something you can teach others. Now it's time for you to start believing that.

Still no clue about what you can write about? Here's a question for ya: "Can you learn more about any given subject?" Maybe you love cats. Can you learn everything there is to know about 'cat behavior'? Of course you can. Can you share what you've learned? Of course you can. It requires work, but don't ever think it's not possible.

The only thing stopping you is your mind. Limiting beliefs about what's possible and about the value you have to share. What's already 'normal, logic or common sense to you, might be completely new to someone else. Don't rob someone else from the pleasure to learn from you. It's nothing to be embarrassed or scared about.

Sure not everyone will be willing to buy your products. Even best selling authors and entrepreneurs face that problem. Look for something you can teach or you have a feeling for. You can research it online and do the work others are not willing to do. Remember; if it adds value people are willing to pay you for it.

Again, you don't have to be a writer. I'm not a perfect writer as well (far from it). There will probably be grammatical errors in this book or sentences that make no sense. But to be honest, it doesn't matter. It's about the message and the value in that message. If people are helped by your content, it sincerely does not matter how they receive it. Doing your best, is good enough.

Ok, on to the next product type you can create.

- **Create a video training**

Have you seen those videos shot on an iPhone? They look amazing. Just for fun, check out some clips created on an iPhone. You'll be amazed. Google 'movies shot on an iPhone'. Some of them look like professional movies.
If you want to create a video with your iPhone I would recommend not using the build-in camera app, but to download a (semi) professional one. I use the app 'Filmic pro' for instance. Google 'how to make video's on your iPhone' and you'll have your own studio in no time. Record yourself talking about any subject you want to talk about.

When you think about subjects to create content about, remember this: 'If you would find the content useful, it's most likely others will as well.' I recommend using a microphone for the sound. It makes the video a lot better. Although I'm not covering how to create these video's in this book, there are tons of resources online.

One more tip, please get to the point fast. It's crucial you don't start talking randomly about yourself or about the subject you're covering. People will tune out before you even got your message across. I'll talk a little bit more about this in the 'generating traffic' chapter.

- **Create an audio training or audiobook**

The way you can write a book, you can also create an audiobook or audio training. Or maybe you can write it first and than narrate it? So you have both! You can offer the option for people to listen or read. You can upload it to audible or any other audio-platform.

You will always have potential customers that don't like reading but love listening and vice-versa. It's highly recommended to create an audio of any written content. I **believe the 'audio-trend' will continue and more and more people will start listening to content instead of reading.**

- **Develop a simple but useful app**

This one might sound weird, but there's billion dollar industry here. There are people like you and me making money with them. If you have an idea for a (simple) app, you can hire a developer from freelancer.com or upwork.com to create it for you. You can upload it to the iPhone or Android store and you're good to go. You are selling an app.

Of course you'll have to create an app that **adds value**. I keep repeating that, but it's crucial. If you would use it, there are probably more people that want to use it. You'll also need to market your app of course. Which I don't cover in this book, but there are some great programs that will help you create an app or even an app business.

I wouldn't start with this, but it is a very viable option later down the road.

Affiliate products

This is particularly easier than creating a product. This is where you take someone else's product(s) and you sell them on your website. You get paid a commission for every sale you do. Commissions can go up to 80% of the sale price. Great right?

There's also a downside. It's great to get started and earn some extra income. But for creating a long lasting, sustainable business, it's better to create products yourself. That way affiliates can sell your products and in the end it will be much more lucrative to grow your business.

That being said, it's a great way to start. You can get some income going and people will love you for referring them to good products. So how do you do this? Depending on the country you're in, there are 'affiliate platforms'. I live in the Netherlands where we use platforms like paypro.nl. But there's also a global one called clickbank.com.

There you can find a lot of products to sell and receive commissions for. They also have very good resources to show you how they work. It will take time to learn how everything works. But as I said, this is a very good option to get started. It will save you a lot of time and effort, since you don't have to create a product, process sales or even have a website.

I would recommend to choose whether you want to create a product or go for affiliate products and stick to that. You can always do something else later. This is really important, because focus is really important in this line of work. If you want my opinion, go for affiliating first. It will give you momentum and you can start building your own products in the process.

I remember myself constantly going back and forth on the choice whether to create a product or promote someone else's. I decided to create one, because I wanted it to be mine, but I could not get it done. I felt the product had to be the best in the industry and I was constantly overwhelmed by that demand and pressure I put on myself. So that get me no step closer to finishing it.

I switched to affiliates and it worked for me. It's really good to get some revenue going and once your business is up and running, you can create your own product. Affiliate products are simply the easier way and if you have a website, or even an email-list already, you can start selling today!

You pick a product to sell, you get your own affiliate link and all the traffic will be tracked with a tracking cookie automatically. Any sale made, will earn you the commission the seller is giving.

I recommend going through Clickbank's great resource database to learn how it works. They can also help you setup campaigns and increase conversions. (A conversion is someone that see's your offer and ends up buying it).

Always make sure you promote high quality products, which can be discovered through reviews and testimonials. You can ask the supplier a sample of their product. Say you want to promote it, but want to check it first.

I highly recommend to take your time researching products and picking products that are high quality and suit your market. This means it's congruent with your own business (or business ideas) and it will not harm you in the future.

For instance if your business will be about online marketing and you decide to promote products in real estate, it will harm your business in the future. The same goes for promoting products that are not up to your standards. You will lose trust and credibility from your followers and it's a disaster for future business.

Online freelancing

Freelancing is great to earn some money and it's incredibly easy nowadays. If you have a skill, you can start making money today. Perhaps you are good at video-editing, writing, drawing, designing or photoshop, you can monetize that skill right now. There are thousands of people looking for you.

The downside is the business aspect. There isn't really any. It's working an x amount of time and receiving an x amount of money for that. Nothing wrong with it, but not really scalable. For me personally this isn't a great option, because I want to create passive income. Not having to work gives me the freedom to do what I want, when I want it.

I would rather create systems, put them in place and generate revenue from them. But having said that, this is by far the fasted and easiest way to make a quick buck. If your main concern is money, than this might be your first choice.

Go to freelancer.com or upwork.com and create an account. Start bidding on small projects and offer a low price. Put some work in your profile, where you explain you are starting out and are willing to work for lower prices, in exchange for a fair review.

Once you've done some projects, you have a portfolio to showcase. Also you've gathered some useful reviews. Now you can start bidding on larger and higher paid projects. It's common sense really.

Although not covering in detail how to create an freelancer account and get work, don't let that stop you. Take my word for it, if you want to earn some cash quick, do this. Go to those websites, read a little bit, consult their resources and you'll be up and running in no time.

Please don't make the mistake thinking it's hard and you can't do it. You can. You have nothing to lose. If this seems viable to you or you need to earn some income quick, this is a solid choice.

Personally I would recommend if you choose to do this, to start building a business on the side. If you're good at photoshop, you can start freelancing but also start creating your business. Follow this book on creating a website/blog and build a portfolio. You can create some awesome tutorials or 'how to' material on your blog.

Later you can create some video training or audio content on specific skills or knowledge. Yes this takes time, but think about it. There will always be people that want to learn. The more value you add, the more money you earn.

Internet marketing format

The world champion of internet marketing formats

Let me show you a format, taught and used by the elite internet marketers out there. This is not just any format, it's a process that has took me years and years to put together. You might be fooled with it's simplicity, but don't be.

To me this is literally the world champion of internet marketing formats. And I've tested this so many times, I am convinced it will always work if you execute it right.

If you want something that works, this is it. I stick to this format for all my products and services. Here is the format, from start to finish, without you having to invest a lot of time and money to learn it.

You might not understand everything at first, but I will explain everything. If some words raise questions, don't worry. I'll explain them all to you.

Here it is:

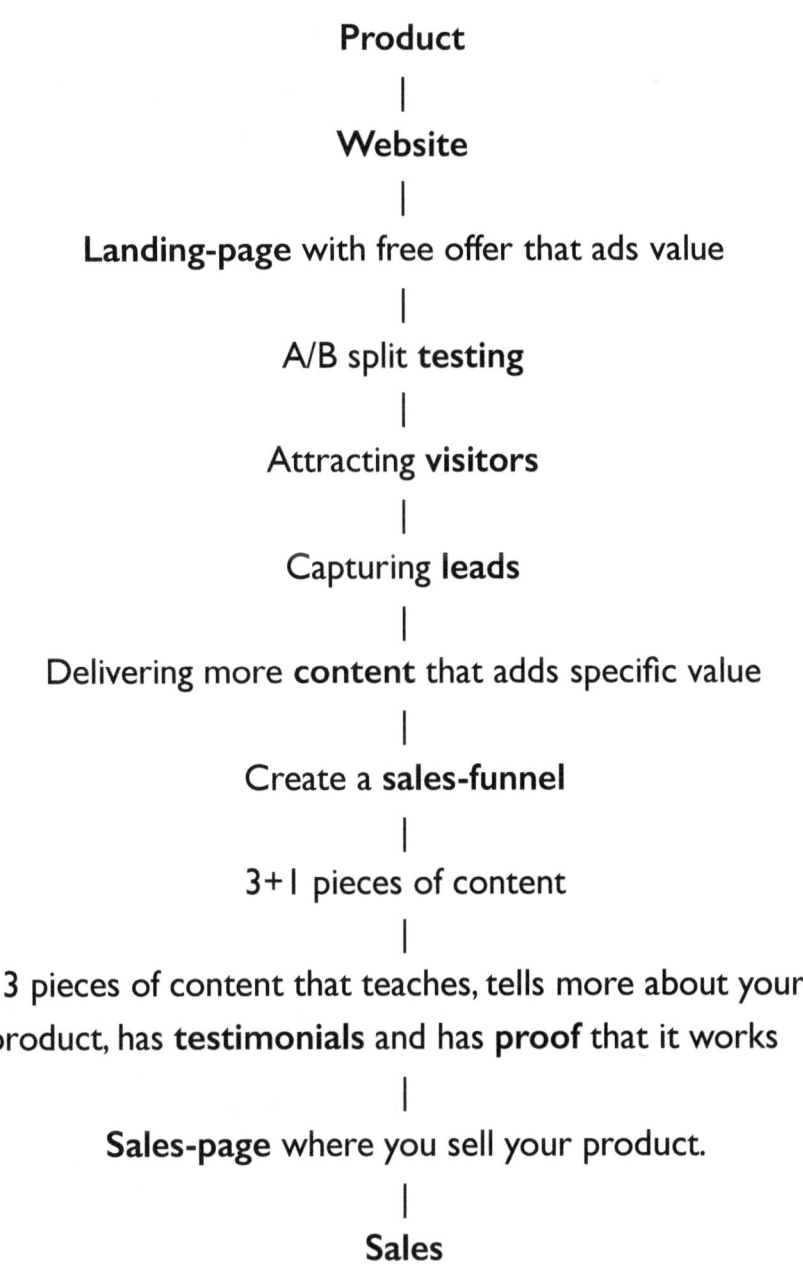

Product

|

Website

|

Landing-page with free offer that ads value

|

A/B split **testing**

|

Attracting **visitors**

|

Capturing **leads**

|

Delivering more **content** that adds specific value

|

Create a **sales-funnel**

|

3+1 pieces of content

|

3 pieces of content that teaches, tells more about your product, has **testimonials** and has **proof** that it works

|

Sales-page where you sell your product.

|

Sales

In the next chapters I'll be covering the next parts of this blueprint. If this doesn't make much sense right now, don't worry. This little blueprint is used by all great internet marketeers, trust me on that. It might be slightly different from time to time, but the essence will be the same.

Your own website

On your own website and how to get it

Moving on to step 2. We finished covering step 1, which was about; creating/finding a product or service to sell. Once you've chosen what to do when it comes to selling, you need somewhere to sell it from.

Step 2: Get a website

You might already have one or several, but if you don't it's very easy to get one. I won't cover building a professional website. But I'll show you how to get going and where to find the things you need to build one. Depending on your goal, there are a lot of options.

One of the platforms you build a good website on is Wordpress, I definitely recommend it. I use Wordpress for everything and feel like I don't need anything else. The downside is that you often need to stay in the 'restraints' of a theme or framework.

This means not everything can be customized. But I personally don't mind. It's easy, customizable enough, professional and has everything you need to market and sell products or services. If you would like to know how to build a Wordpress website, let me know. If more people want to know I'll create a separate kindle book on that topic.

Here is the minimum you need to get started:

- A Wordpress account. Wordpress is not the only option you have. But I think it's great and the easiest and fastest way to build a website.
- You need hosting. Every website is 'hosted' by a hosting company. Without it, you can't be online.
- You need to register a domain. Think long term with your domain. Don't worry too much about it. If you don't know what to choose, go for you name. And stick to .com .net or .org. You have plenty of options nowadays, but I would stick to those if you can. They're the most trustworthy.

These are the options I use and where to find them:

- For your website: www.wordpress.com
    - Theme: Optimize press; www.optimizepress.com
- For your hosting: www.hostgator.com
- Domains: www.godaddy.com
- Email service: Activecampaign; www.activecampaign.com

This is cheap, fast and it works! For now, if you want to know more, look it up online. Also let me know if you need details, I will always be willing to help. Most tutorials can be simply found online and these brands all have good resources.

With a little bit effort, you can learn it yourself. There is a lot of free content available about these topics. If you are in any way serious about changing your life and building an online business, start with your website right now. Go to Wordpress.com and start learning. If you put in some time, you'll have you website up and running in a few days. It doesn't have to be fancy, all it needs is some effort and to first actually be created!

Many people believe you need a shit load of content on your website, you don't. You have to show you are a real person, a real business with real content. But in order to start selling a product or service, you only have to be 'trustworthy'. Yes, loads of useful (on-topic) content helps with that. But it's not a necessity.

If you are building your website, make sure you show yourself. People want to see a real person, not a shady business. The first thing you can do is share a short story about you and what your website will be about. It helps with your credibility.

By now you should have started on your website. It's not done, I know. It will never be 'done'. Just get going already!

You are taking action and you are on your way! Great.

By the way, there are more ways people will see you as trustworthy. For instance; social media, seeing you on video or hearing your voice. If you are sincere and create value, people will most likely recognize that. The easiest way to earn someone's trust is a video. Let people see you and be yourself.

If you are not that good on video, than create an audio. Where you explain who you are, what you do and what people will find with you. I have three valuable tips when it comes to video and audio and they make or break succeeding with them:

1) Being sincere
2) Energy/enthusiasm
3) Letting people know what's in it

Thousands of people make the mistake of 'just talking' in an audio or video. With all the content online these days, how long before people will get bored? If you just start talking it will be an average of 5 seconds before they are gone. These tips truly matter. You will never see an online professional not doing these three things, trust me.

Tip #1 is obvious, be sincere and be yourself.

Tip #2 is energy. Hype yourself up and be enthusiastic. It's contagious and listeners will feel it. If you are enthusiastic about the video, it's most likely they will be too. Also it's much more fun/enticing to watch.

Tip #3 Never forget to state what the video is about exactly. You always start with something like this:

"Hi I'm .... from .....com,
In this short video I'll be covering 1-2-3 and how you can 1-2-3"

It's very easy, but it makes a massive difference. If people know what's coming and it's valuable to them, they will most likely stay. People get more and more picky with watching or listening to content online so make sure you do that.

I'm going slightly off topic here, but these things are important. If you are reading this you should really have your website and some content on your topic. Feel free to peak at erikpenders.com and see how I do it. You can see what my website is about in 1 second, right?

You cannot copy content of course, but you can copy strategies. Now, you can keep reading, but it would best if you started on your website by now. If you haven't; do it now. So you can benefit from the coming chapters.

Generating traffic/visitors

On attracting visitors

Before we go into strategies to get these visitors, I first want to talk about the people that come to your website. You don't 'just' send people to your website. You need a plan if you want your visitors to turn into customers. Before you send any visitor to your website, you need to be able to receive them properly.

We call these people, leads. A lead is a visitor interested in your content or what it is you're promoting. I.o.w:

Visitors/leads are potential customers.

You should see every visitor to your website as a potential customer. Which means you should try to find a way to keep in contact with them, after they leave your website. We do this by offering them free, valuable content, in exchange for their name and/or email address.

So called 'optins' are a great way of doing that. Despite what anyone might tell you, optins work and will continue to work for years to come. As long as you get a few things right. Email is not dead, email is very much alive and it will be for a long time.

People are however, much more skeptical now than they were 10 years ago. Information overload hits everyone nowadays and people receive so much offers, it's hard for them to separate value over crap. The solution is quite simple.

Your content must add massive value to your <u>target</u> audience.

This is the only crucial part. You can have a beautifully designed website, great graphics, great sales pitches and copy, but if you do not add massive value, you're bound to fail. For me it works really well to ask the following question:

What problems does my audience have and how do I help solve them in the best way?

It's often best to base your whole content on those kind of questions. Your content will be picked up if it's valuable, it's that simple. So there are numerous of ways to get visitors and before I share them with you, first we need a place to send our visitors so we can collect their contact information and stay in touch.

You get the idea for 'capturing' these leads. I will explain it a little bit more in detail a little later. First, let's dive in to the traffic strategies

Traffic

The best way to create ongoing and valuable traffic, is your content. The more value in your content, the more value will be coming from your visitors. What I mean is that uninterested, unengaged visitors will probably leave within seconds and they are not valuable to you.

We are looking for real, engaged and ready to buy visitors. This means you should never try to trick someone to come to your website. This includes bribing, buying or stealing traffic. This might sound ludicrous, but it happens. Never under any circumstance lose your dignity by doing these things. It will never ever build a real sustainable business.

Instead, always be honest, sincere and open, in all the content you put out there. Have the balls to show yourself and who you are. It's ok to be aggressive at times with your marketing and promotions. It's part of your business. Try to make sure that all your content is congruent with your message.

What are you about? What are you sharing? Why are you worth their time? Answer those questions first, before using any of the coming strategies. Determining these things will greatly help your content and communication. Now let me show you how to actually 'get' traffic.

Now step 3 will be using one or all of the 'traffic generating' strategies. Very important is to measure your traffic. You can use google analytics for that. Install it on your website and track your traffic.

Step 3: Use one or more of the traffic generating strategies, track your traffic and create your first thousand visitors.

Let's get in to these strategies.

Organic strategy

Organic traffic is traffic that comes to your website 'naturally' through search engines. It's free traffic that requires no specific strategy. Organic traffic is less useful than it used to be in my opinion, especially short term. Long term it works really well, but you don't necessarily need a strategy for that. It's about content creation.

There are better ways to flood your website with traffic right now. The only reason I receive organic visitors is because I write content, place it on my website, with the sole purpose to enhance any existing relationship with potential customers and add value for them.

Now despite creating content and adding value for your audience, the real traffic comes from SEO(search engine optimization). A strategy how to use SEO to get traffic will be post on my blog. It's to detailed to explain it here. But if you want organic traffic, you need an SEO strategy. If you don't, a lot of good pieces of content will not be read.

I do want to give you a general explanation how it works. You optimize content for certain 'keywords'. Keywords are certain words or combination of words on which content will be found by search engines. For instance, if you have content about long haired cats, people that search for 'long haired cats' might find your content by searching for that word.

Your content should be 'optimized' for one (or max a few) keyword. This means it should be mentioned in the title, meta tag, url and several times inside the content.

Be aware to never try to 'trick' google in sending you traffic. It's a strategy that's bound to bite you in the ass in the long run. It doesn't work, period. Instead of that, look at it this way: If you write valuable content on a certain subject, that actually helps people, google will send you traffic. That's the basis.

The more content you create, the more value that content brings to the marketplace, he more relevant the content is and the better your SEO strategy is, the more traffic your website will get.

Youtube strategy

This strategy is one of the most effective strategies I have ever seen, no joke. This can bring you so much traffic, you never saw it coming. Let me explain how this works.

Video is very popular as you might know. Search engines also really like video. Which makes ranking a video about 800x more likely to get ranked than written content. How incredible is that? So let me show you how to use video for your website.

Imagine you want to create a piece of content about a certain subject. Let's use a sample subject, so you understand what I mean. We'll use dog hair trimming. (No idea why, but it sounds funny) If you make a piece of content, you can always turn that into a video.

You can use an iPhone to video yourself or record your voice and put some images underneath. There's ton of resources on how you can create video's or even hire people to do it for you. A Narrater for instance, to speak on your video. Websites like freelancer.com or upwork.com have a lot of freelancers that can do work for you.

Once you've created your video, it's time to upload it to video-websites. I believe uploading your video to these website is common sense, it's not hard. This book is not about these details, but if you need help google this: 'how to upload my video to youtube', you will find detailed information on how to do that.

For this example we'll use youtube, but I recommend uploading to as many video-websites as you can find. (Google 'video sites', or 'website to upload video's') When you upload the video, follow this exact sequence:

1. Google key word optimizer. This is a service google provides where you can check the traffic for certain keywords. Check google for resources on how it works. Fill in your keyword(s), what your video is about. Check the traffic and competition of these keywords. The so-called 'long tail' often has less competition. A long tail can be described as a 'longer' keyword. For instance the keywords 'cats', to the long tail keyword 'longhaired cats on the street'. I would recommend to find a long tail keyword in your market, with enough traffic but less competition. Keep in mind that's it's a lot easier to rank with a video, so don't worry about a little bit of competition.
2. The (long-tail) keyword you found in your research, should be the title of the video.
3. Put a link to your landing page in the FIRST line of the description of the video

4. Use the google key word tool to find additional keyword to add to your video. Of course all keywords have to be relevant to your main subject.
5. Before you choose anything, fill out your keyword in youtube and see how many video's you find and if there are some with a decent amount of views. If so, you know you're on the right track
6. Upload the video

Be a little bit creative as well. That's what business is all about. Are there other ways to research a market or keyword?

Facebook strategy

I believe Facebook is best used for three things: Engagement with your content or brand, social interaction and advertising. Engagement is great, so posting engaging content like images with text in them or fun video's is great for that goal. But I don't see it as a highly effective strategy.

I hardly ever see a piece of content or video go viral by itself and create an impact. I would much rather be strategic about it, than try to post random content and hope it hits. What's important on Facebook is to show that your brand or your content is 'alive'.

What I mean is that a constant stream of (useful/fun) content and interaction really helps to show you are real, your brand or content is real and it's live and happening right now. There's actually some handy software to help you plan ahead with posts on social media. Like Hootsuite. (Google it to learn more)

Now there is one thing I want to give some more attention, because that's actually a great strategy for creating high value visitors. Facebook advertising.

Yes, you need to spend a bit of money for that. But it will be a lot less than you think and I will show you ways to optimize your advertising to decrease your cost and increase conversions. You can create a lot of leads for dollar-cents, no joke. With just a few dollars, you can have awesome results.

If the rest of your system is in place, you will earn this money back tenfold. Again I cannot go into too much detail, I need to stay on topic. But I will give you some quick pointers. Only start using Facebook advertising if you actually have something to sell. Use a sales funnel for that, as explained in that chapter.

Without telling you how to set up Facebook advertising and using it (Please refer to Facebook's resources on this), I will tell you that you can create different 'kind' of advertisements. In my experience the best ads are 'posts'. This is a particular way of creating ads.

It's basically writing a post like you usually do and then turn it into an ad. Because you can use more text and images I believe this to be the best advertisement possibility. I've had the best results with these kind of ads. When you create a post and you decide to advertise it, remember that you should send people to a landing page, with an opt-in offer there.

Make sure the opt-in offer resonates with your post, so there's a big chance that people will be interested in your opt-in offer. In Facebook you can target very specific groups and I very much recommend choosing a target audience.

You can select specific age groups, gender, countries, area they live and even what they like. For instance if you write about weight loss, you can go for women, between 25-45, living in the area with highest obesity rates maybe, and they like your type of workout or fitness. You can get all that just from Facebook.

Leads and building a database

Capturing leads

Whatever you're promoting or selling, collecting leads is a game changer. It's always been this way and it will not change. Too many online businesses assume that having a product is enough. It's not. If you want to have the best results you need to have a proven system. Collecting leads is a crucial part in that system.

If you want to have the highest conversions(the amount of people that are interested in your content and end up buying from you) you cannot skip this part.

People are much more likely to buy from someone or something they know, like and trust.

Collecting leads is like the basis of building a relationship with your (potential) customer before you ever try to sell them anything. This is only possible if you can contact them and share valuable content with them. Content they are interested in.

Ok, so how do you get people to leave there contact information with you? We do that with what we call: 'the optin offer'. You offer something for free with great value and ask for their contact-information in return. If your offer is good, people will signup. Who doesn't want value for free, right?

I recommend keeping it small, valuable and really help solve a problem. People are often not willing to read whole books or watch a video that's too long. Quick and awesome content works best.

For instance, if you're in the weight loss industry. I would offer something like: '5 new ways to shed body fat today.' Or in the internet business: 5 hacks to get 2400 visitors to your website within 2 days. Etc. You get the point.

These kind of offers sometimes sound sleazy, but they work. They solve a problem and they do it fast. The important thing here, is that the actual content people receive after they leave their name and/or email, has to be so good and actually solve the problem they face. People need to feel they really got something valuable from you. Most people go wrong here. Personally, I always try to:

Over-deliver on the optin-offer, the perceived value should be greater than expected.

Your first impression should last with your prospects (potential customers). So go the extra mile there and you will establish a foundation for a long term relationship. For your 'optin-content' you can record a short video of yourself, write a pdf, a short audiobook, whatever you want. Again, give them more than what they signed up for.

You can show visitors these optin-offers in multiple ways. You often see an optin in the right side bar or at the end of content. Sometimes they pop up (called a lightbox) when you scroll through content. Or sometimes they even pop up when you want to leave the page. Although these are all fine options, the biggest conversions will be made with a landing page.

Step 4: Create a free optin offer that truly adds value. Make it high quality and preferably use a landing page.

Landing pages

You've probably seen a landing page before. It's a page that offers free content in exchange for their email address, on a page with no content whatsoever, only an offer and an optin. The page is only about the free content offered.

As I mentioned in the previous chapter, these pages convert better than other optin options, so I highly recommend using one. If you start advertising for instance, you really want to send people to a landing page. That way your cost will give the highest return on the dollar.

After all you are paying for traffic and you want to get the most value out of these visitors. Value is created by capturing email addresses and selling to them later. We establish a relationship with them. They know, like and trust you and that's when they will buy from you.

Go to https://images.google.com/ and type in 'landing page examples'. Here you see how a landing page looks. Some convert better than others. You have to test that. This is called an A/B or split test, which I'll explain in the next chapter.

A landing page is one of the easiest pages to create. As you can see in the examples, it's one page with one offer. Although it's simple do not underestimate this page and spend enough time for your offer. Try to think and feel like your audience. What are they looking for, what are their problems, fears and frustrations. Which of those things is most pressing and urgent? How can you help solve their problem?

If you get this right, you will lay the foundation of your business.

A/B or split testing

This basically means testing two landing pages and see which one converts better. Once you know, you pick one. Create an alternative landing page with some tweaks on it and test again. You repeat this process until you find a landing page that converts optimal.

It's hard to say what's 'optimal' for you. Conversion rates differ from market to market and depend on hundreds of factors. You'll get a feel for it, as long as you test it you are on the right track.

How do you do that? How do you create a landing page, options and test them? First of all, I'm no techie. I have no idea how to do this manually and I only have a general idea of how coding works. Luckily there are plenty of people that created solutions to these problems.

I will show you the right direction, but again I cannot go in to detail on how to create them. At least not in this book. I'll be sure to create content on these topics if it's needed by more people. I really want to help you create your online business. Let me show you what I do.

So first I learned how to use Wordpress. Once that's covered I went looking for resources on landing pages, optin templates and other useful tools for optimizing conversions. After testing a billion things, I ended up with this plugin: **Thrive leads**. They have all sorts of cool landing page templates, optin templates and testing options. Also easily integrated with mail services like a-weber and Mailchimp.

Also nice to know, I use a (paid) framework for wordpress called 'optimize press'. I've been using that for years and it let's you create custom websites and they have all sorts of cool internet marketing options.

How to do sales and increase conversions

The sales funnel

A sales funnel is a specific combination of content you put your prospect (potential customer) through. This content is optimized and made for selling. It's often presented in a particular order so it will make the product irresistible for the prospect.

What works really well is not just directing your audience towards a sales page. Actually create custom, valuable content, that teaches your audience. Where any more 'in depth' training or content is your product. Video is widely used for this strategy and it works really well. It goes like this.

A first email is send out, which states that some amazing free content is up if you're interested and you can check it out. You land on a page with a big video player and 4 boxes below.

The first box reads video 1: Playing now. (This one is playing on the video player) The second box reads Video 2: Coming soon. The third box read: Video 3: Coming soon and the fourth also. I would love to give an image as example, but in this kindle book I will be using images. Still I think you get the point.

You can use these video's or content how you would like to, but I've tested the following format and it works really well:

- The first video/content will be used to learn the prospect something awesome that has something to do with the product you are selling.
- The second video/content is used to show some awesome features of the product and perhaps even see it in action
- The third video/content is used to show testimonials and other people using the product with great endorsements.
- The fourth is your sales video/content where you will tell your prospect it's their turn and link to your sales page.

In all video's you remind the prospect when the next video will be sent and what is coming, so they'll be enticed not to miss it. This is such an easy strategy, with a little bit of work your conversions will skyrocket.

Sales page

This is where you will sell your product or service. Never underestimate this page, you should have a plan for this page. It increases or decreases your sales, logically. Here I always use the ancient but still very good AIDA model.

Aida, stands for: Attention, Interest, desire, action. A good sales page begins with having an offer that solves someone's problem or problems, it starts with that. After that, you use the Aida model as a framework for your page:

Attention: You begin with a catchy headline where the attention is grabbed of your reader. This is basically the short and enticing version of how you are going to solve your reader's problem. For instance, I have a website but no visitors, that's a problem for me.

If you run into a website with a headline like: "Get 1000 real visitors to your website for free within a week." It's kinda impossible that this would not grab my attention right? Of course it does. Someone has a solution for my problem, great.

Interest: So there you want to turn there attention into interest. You give some additional information, but you keep it short. What really works well here are bullet points with some key factors of your product. So people understand it a little bit more. Like this:

- 3 tested strategies that will not cost a single dime
- Easy to use, it will only take you one hour
- Real and interested visitors, guaranteed.
- Etc.

So here we get some more information about the product or service that will get us really interested. Make sure you are always truthful, you don't want people buying your product and feel disappointed. At least, that's my point of view.

Desire: So now it's time to spike their desire. Here I believe it's smart to try to influence people and go to the emotional level. This means thinking about what it will mean to them once their problem is solved, with your product. Let me give you an example, I might write something like:

- Think about how many more leads, revenue and business you will you create with these strategies.
- The great part is you can repeat these strategies as many times as you want. So what will 1000 potential customers mean to you? Or 2000, or 5000? Are you ready for a massive amount of customers?

So these are just ideas, but as you can imagine, who wouldn't want this to happen right? Slowly but surely you are pulling them in with good copy. After that it's time to make a killer offer.

Action: You want them to take action. This needs to be simple and easy to do. The more barriers we create the lower the chance they will buy from us. Your offer should be perceived as a great deal. One of the tricks many internet marketeers use, is offering an X amount of $ as free bonuses.

So for instance they say the customer they are throwing in a free coaching call, worth 500$. Or a free video training, 200$ etc. The perceived value of your product goes up with this strategy and it becomes much easier to sell it. Again, your product should be very good if you really want to create a lasting business. Now there's one more important strategy we need to use on our sales page. Scarcity.

It really works to make your offer a now or never. For instance put a timer on it and say the price will go after 3 hours. Or say you only have 100 left in stock and they're flying out the door. Again, I want you to be truthful here. Don't create false scarcity, most people will see right through it.

If I want to buy a digital course and the sales pages is stating it only has 20 left in stock, I'm out. It's deceitful, digital products have unlimited stock as we all know. Anyway, you get my point.

Product types

Low, mid and high-end products

What this means is that you have different sizes and prices in products and services. From like 1 tot 20$, to 50-250$, to 250-100.000$. These are not exact numbers, but it gives you an idea of low, mid and high end products and services.

Yes, there are internet marketeers selling their advice for 100 k or more. But if you are a beginner, you don't start there of course. I would definitely recommend beginners to start with low-end products. This means relatively affordable, smaller products, easy scalable.

This doesn't mean you should take it lightly, I've told you over and over, the content needs to be good. I really believe in long-term business and adding value. If you can solve a problem with something simple, like an ebook or a short video training, you are already well on your way.

Once you've established some credibility, like reviews and testimonials and you've earned your respect in a certain field, that's often a good time to create a more expensive product or service. One key factor in being able to sell mid and high end products is 'authority'.

If you establish that in your line of work, than more people will be willing to spend more money on you. Authority basically means that you've proven to be a professional and you know what you're talking about. You are obviously one of the 'experts' in your area.

But there's actually another way to establish the same feeling with your potential customers. It's called 'perceived authority'. You can position yourself as an authority rather easy these days, without being deceitful. It sounds weird, but it's true.

What if you could become a 'best selling' author in your field? This might sounds impossible, but it's actually not that hard. Let me tell you how in the next part. My 'ninja strategy to establish authority'. This will not only help you do that, but also create a low-end product that you can sell.

On creating instant authority

Ninja strategy to create a product and instant authority

You're going to love this! This is something I've done personally and it works like a charm. So, what's the ninja strategy. Do you know what you're reading right now? A kindle book right?

Did you know you can become a published author and even a best selling author just from uploading a kindle book to amazon. Well of course you need to do some work for it, but anyone and everyone can upload a book to amazon.

I would actually recommend that being your first low-end product. Maybe you think you're not a writer, or think it's hard to do. Well, I wasn't a writer, until I started writing. I just did it and trust me I'm no one special. I just did the work, that's all.

I wrote a short book and put it on kindle. If you work in a specific market or area and you promote your book, it's not that hard to become a best selling author in your niche market. How does that look: Best selling author .... With your name behind it.

Do you know what people think when they read that? That you're an expert and the go-to guy. You've created instant authority without doing years of work.

Mindset and motivation

About mindset and motivation

This book is created to be a practical guide and show you how to build an online (lifestyle) business. But it lacks what's **probably the most important part of building a business, seriously.**

Without addressing issues concerning your mindset and motivation, it's simply impossible to succeed. Please watch this short video, where I start out with some very important 'mindset' pointers. I've struggled with (and learned about) these issues the most. They are crucial in your success. Giving up, getting distracted, lacking motivation, they are all part of the deal and you will run in to them. It's wise to learn about it and have a strategy to master these issues.

Here's the video: https://www.youtube.com/watch?v=jYzuCnuWZss

If you cannot use the link, go the my website and find it there: erikpenders.com. As I mentioned before, there's a lot more about building your business, but also mindset and motivation on my website. Make sure to visit me there if you want to know more.

Closing word

10 steps from nothing to business

Remember the format I showed you? Let's look back and see what you need to start building your own business right now. And see that it really isn't that hard to do. This what you need from A to Z in a slightly different order:

1) Product; Affiliate with Clickbank and pick high a quality product on your subject
|
2) Website; Create a website with Wordpress and add an email optin
|
3) Attracting visitors; Content, content, content. Write blog posts and create video's that add value
|
4) Capturing leads; Using email optins on your home page and landing-page.
|
5) More content that adds specific value; Content, content, content.
|
6) Create a sales-funnel; Build people up to the product your selling with free, valuable content
|

7) 3+1 pieces of content in your sales funnel.

|

8) 3 pieces of content that teaches, tells more about your product, has testimonials and proof that it works

|

9) Sales-page where you sell your product.

|

10) Sales

Don't make it harder than it is, follow this format and you will be building your own online successful business.

Thanks!

Thank you for reading this book. I truly promise you this book works. Whatever you want to sell, this is the way to go. If you have any questions or you want to have some more information don't hesitate to contact met at info@erikpenders.com.

Don't forget to signup on my website to learn more. If you are up for it, I will teach you everything I've learned and you can copy it all to start your own online (lifestyle) business. http://www.erikpenders.com is where to find me.

I would love for you to give me an honest review on amazon. These reviews really help me. If this is helpful for you I hope you are willing to do that for me. Thanks a lot! Take care and good luck on your own online business journey.

Erik

www.ingramcontent.com/pod-product-compliance
Lightning Source LLC
Chambersburg PA
CBHW070333190526
45169CB00005B/1868